The Miracle Already Happening

everyday life with Rumi

Poems by

Rosemerry Wahtola Trommer

Liquid Light Press
Premium Chapbook First Edition

ISBN: 978-0-9836063-1-4

Liquid Light Press

poetry that speaks to the heart

www.liquidlightpress.com

Back Cover Photo of Rosemerry by Darby Ullyatt

Cover Photo by Rosemerry Wahtola Trommer

Cover Design by M. D. Friedman

Preface

It was fall. Santa Barbara. 2010. And Rumi, the Sufi poet, was hanging out with a roomful of cheerleaders. At least he was in a poem I heard that afternoon by fellow poet, Barry Spacks.

That joint reading at the Mission began an enduring poetic camaraderie with Barry. It also began a new friendship of sorts with Rumi. Inspired by Barry's anachronism and playfulness, I began to envision the 13th century mystic waxing ecstatic about union with the beloved while I was in my son's kindergarten classroom, at the beach or at karate. And everywhere I am able to picture Rumi, he shows me where I'm closed-minded, judgmental, or stuck and suggests new ways to see the world.

The "friendship" isn't channeling, of course. It's literature based. I've long enjoyed Rumi on the page. I've memorized translations by Coleman Barks and Daniel Ladinsky so I might have Rumi's poems with me while hiking or preserving pears. I've devoured books about Rumi's life and led discussion groups on his works. Since that Santa Barbara afternoon, however, I've related to Rumi's words less as literature and more as intimate conversation.

Obviously, the "friendship" is mainly fueled by imagination. As my friend Wendy Videlock says, "You do not use the imagination. It uses you." My imaginary Rumi has been helping me laugh at myself. A lot. Here he is, even now, smiling as I struggle to write a preface. "Forget yourself," he might say. "And remember God."

Why Rumi? Andrew Harvey writes in *The Way of Passion: A Celebration of Rumi*, "I suggest that your heart is hungry to hear news about your true identity, about your Divine origin, about the splendor and glory of that origin, and about the splendor and glory of the world as revealed in the eye of the heart, in the sight of the true and awakened heart." Oh yes, says my heart. Famished. Yours, too?

The real Rumi, with his revelations of Divine love, invites each of us to remember our own sacredness, initiating us into the ecstasy and responsibility that come with it. Because I write poems, that's how Rumi comes to me. Perhaps as you read Rumi—there are so many of his beautiful poems to read—you will find that he somehow comes alive in your hungry heart, too. And in your kitchen, your car, your office ...

Note from the poet:

In the following poems, the Rumi quotes in italics are Rumi's own words, reprinted here with the generous permission of translators, Coleman Barks and Daniel Ladinsky. Full permissions corresponding to each poem are printed in the back of the book.

Any Rumi quotes punctuated with quotation marks stem from my imagination.

The Miracle Already Happening

everyday life with Rumi

Rumi in the Garden

Be nothing,
says Rumi,
and I say,

"But ..."
I am thinning
the carrots,

crowded in the row,
and I wonder
who will thin them

if I am nothing.
"I did not say
do nothing,"

he says. *Be nothing.*
"But ..." I say.
The soil

is damp and
the carrots pull
easily from the earth,

their bright orange
roots already thick
enough to eat.

They are sweet,
and I offer
one to Rumi

who eats it
dirt and all.
Be a spot of ground

where nothing
is growing, he says,
where something

might be planted.
He tosses the greens
to the ground.
I look between
my hands to the nothing
beneath the greens

and perhaps
for a moment
I feel what he means,

but too soon
a thought
of knowing comes in

and there I go
being something
again.

Rumi Goes to the Beach

I didn't really want
to walk into the ocean.
Though the breeze was warm.

Though the water was clear.
Being dry felt, well, so dry.
And I liked it, feeling dry.

"You can't be baptized
if you don't get in the water,"
said Rumi, and he rushed

past me from behind, leaping,
launching himself into the waves.
Then he turned toward shore to splash me.

"But the water's so ... wet,"
I said, with a wince.
And he splashed me again.

And he splashed me again.
And I did not did not like it.
I scowled and used my foot to splash

Rumi back, but he already
was wholly glittering wet.
He just laughed and motioned

for me to come deeper in.
I didn't want to go, so I can't quite
explain why I did, except

there was somehow a larger part of me
already at play in the waves with him,
and it pulled in the smaller,

resistant part until all of my limbs
were diamonding in the sun. The ocean
smoothed me with lavish salts

and brought jellyfish to bloom
at my side. Rumi, he had
long since melted into the waves.

His breath was the ocean's breath.
The white gulls creeeched and keeled
overhead, and for a moment I felt

such compassion for that fussy one
who was tying up her wind-licked hair,
hoping to keep at least that part dry.

Less

I want to be more.
To be the rain in the desert.
To be nectar.

To grow wings. And every door
I open, I imagine I could open
it wider. I want to be

not just the sunrise, but a better
sunrise. Not just a woman,
but a better woman. Not just

a song, but the whole symphony.
To open the door is not enough.
I want to take the door off

its hinges, to take down the walls, too.
See what a reaching mind can do?
It will tear down the whole house

just to let in a breeze.
"Oh friend," says Rumi,
from behind the sunrise,

A parrot falls in love with an Arabian colt.
Fish want linen shirts. The drunken
lions hunt drunken gazelles.

I try to be not just a good listener,
but the best listener, and lean
toward him so far I fall down

on my ear. "My dear," Rumi says,
the prayer rugs all point different ways.
What is he trying to say? Which way

would he have me turn? And should
I buy a rug? *Morning opens a door with help*
he says, *for those who don't ask for any.*

My long list of wants appears in the sky
like a murmuration of starlings moving in,
strangely attached to me, crowding out the sun.

I wonder what would happen
if I could cut loose even one
of these 10,000 tethers?

Rather to Be Hiking on the Mountaintop, But

*Look ... Reality is greater than the sum of its parts, also a damn sight
holier. ... For focus simply move a few inches back or forward. And
once more ... look.*
         —Ken Kesey, *Sometimes a Great Notion*

Waiting for an hour
beside the Walmart parking lot,
one hundred degrees and rising,

it is easy to believe that nothing
is holy. Not the asphalt, not the floral flip-flops
on the shuffling feet that pass,

not the gum on our soles nor the cigarette butts
that litter the concrete gutter. Harder to believe
that everything leads us toward god——even

this vast emptiness inside me, some place
I have tried to pave over, have tried to fill with post-its and notebooks,
have tried to scurry across or write off as a wasteland.

There is birdsong everywhere, everywhere a window of sky,
and here, even shade——oh thank you——a shadow
on a small plot of grass where a woman might rest

long enough to see she is not at all separate
from the asphalt, the cumulonimbus expanding above,
the gutter, the half-spent butts. Car fumes

and brown thirsting grass. How awkward
to be part of it all—even that which I'd rather not see.
I imagine what Rumi might say, or the Buddha,

or even Ken Kesey, and know they would find what is holy
right here. You have got to be kidding, I say to myself,
while in my gut blossoms a new kind of prayer.

Rumi Goes to Kindergarten

And when Miss Lackey says, "Children,
this is so sad. Someone
left the lid off of the marker,

and we know how valuable they are,"
Rumi raises his hand and says,
September is a time for death.

Do you think death is a bad thing?
And Miss Lackey tips her head
in an inquisitive way, as she does,

and then kneels down close to him.
"Did you do it?" Miss Lackey asks Rumi.
"Did you leave the lid off the black pen?"

He smiles. "Your work is not to point
to who's to blame, rather to find
all the boxes you put around the way

you think things should be."
Miss Lackey gives him a lopsided smile.
"Rumi, do you mean me?"

She sends the rest of the kids to recess.
Meanwhile Rumi sits in his chair.
"You're a funny one Rumi,"

Miss Lackey says. "I'm a fool,"
he says, jumps on the table
and starts to spin. "Five more minutes,"

says Miss Lackey. And Rumi grins.

Even Realizing This, I Still Google "Rumi, Sweetness, Scattering"

Oh Rumi, already
I have forgotten

your words from
this morning. I heard

them as though through
a hundred white veils.

It was something
about sweetness

and scattering, and
it feels like a loss

not to remember
exactly what was said.

Your words
were like, I don't know,

a breeze moving over
my body, rearranging me

as if I were sand, so
that what remains is

more art of the beloved and
something less of me.

Perhaps this is part
of the letting go—

unleashing the mind of words,
even lovely ones,

as the body releases
a breath, remembering

how lungs do not lament
the air that so marvelously,

so briefly made them full.

Nine New Windows

This being human is a guesthouse.
Every morning a new arrival.
                    —Rumi

i.

Today I read that in Italy,
the gesture for mourning
is clapping. Like the trees did
today in the wind as I walked
while I wept, practicing
the gesture for sorrow that I know best.

ii.

It was a bird I'd never seen before.
The head so red, the wings
so slight. I did not want to catch it
nor hold it nor cage it nor even
give it a name. I wanted only
to watch it as long as I could
and listen for its voice.

iii.

In the driveway, beneath the elm,
half a tiny white egg shell,
cracked open and still so soft.

iv.

Let's say fear is a salesman,
and shame would answer the door.
One keeps knocking.
The other keeps hiding beneath a chair.

v.

Another woman might doubt
that these birds are angels
come to waltz.
I may be filled with gray clouds,
but
I believe in dancing.

vi.

It was a wild applause.
Leaves and the thin green drupes
shaped like long slender, upside down hearts.
How they rattled like laughter on the trees.
I broke one open with the nail of my thumb
and saw how green the seeds,
how soft it was in the center.

vii.

If tears come,
they are a blessing.
Farewell to only
flirting with the world.

viii.

And so I swept the house.
Violently. As if cleaning were salvation.
As if a woman could be made whole
by how shiny her linoleum,
how emptied her space.

ix.

Among sharp pebbles,
a poem dwelt, rich and golden as yolk.
I took off my shoes
and danced.

We Think We Know What It Will Look Like

Standing in the thick green
of bindweed and cheese wheel
it is easy to dream of a time

when the garden is perfectly
hoed and the peppers hang
red on the stems, the green beans

dangle like long slender earrings
and the ears of corn swell with gold.
"Silly dreamer," says Rumi, who

comes in to sit beside the peas.
"You are waiting for a miracle
when it is already happening."

But Am I Ready?

What was said to the rose that made it open was said
to me here in my chest.
                        —Rumi

And who was it that spoke
to the mint seed, encouraging it
to grow and grow and know

itself in every possible setting—
mint in the hard clay, robust
mint in the loam, brisk mint

pushing blithely through
doubled up black weed cloth.
I am now hearing perhaps

the same voice—though it's not
like a voice, more like mint—
sweet, familiar, strong,

obliterating everything I might
plant to compete with it, and my god,
it's everywhere.

Footing

When I walked out of the closet
in brown leather boots
with thick clunky heels
and deep zigzag treads,

Rumi laughed out loud
and from the couch he said,
"My dear, you don't need to wear those."

"But I need something sturdy
and tough," I said,
"to get me through all this muck."

Rumi looked around the room.
"I don't see any muck."
The wooden floors wore a glassy shine.

"Where'd it go?" I wondered, looking around
for the mess I'd skirted for years.

I must have looked disappointed,
having finally brought
the right shoes for a path
that was no longer there.

Rumi smiled. "My dear, you look sweet to me.
Go ahead. Wear the boots. Wear them
until your feet blister and ache,

till your toes are cramped
and your arches scream. Then take off
the boots, and take off your socks,
and come to me again."

Rumi Appears at the Elementary Choir Concert

From the back row, Camille can't see her mom.
The spotlights are too bright and she starts to cry.

On stage left, Suki nervously lifts up
and down her skirt folds of taffeta, red.

Terry's brow is scrunched like a prune.
But most of the kindergarteners stare,

blank as freshly erased chalkboards
waiting to be written on in someone else's hand.

At last, the director hushes the crowd,
turns to the children, and gestures to them to smile.

Some muster a grimace, and the director raises her hands to begin
when Rumi runs across the stage with a tambourine.

"Come stand in front," she says, crossly.
He begins, instead, to dance.

Why look like a dead fish in this ocean of God?
he shouts and spins around the apron.

All the parents watch, hands cupped
to their mouths, wondering whose child he is,

hoping their own child will stand still.
Sing in tune. Bow. And in single file,

follow the director offstage. Meanwhile,
Rumi tosses his tambourine into the crowd,

claps his hands when a parent catches it,
then he goes to the front row to quietly stand,

his real smile resonating around the hall
as only a real smile can.

Sneak Attack

He wore a red cable knit sweater.
He limped. His skin was pitted and sallow.

I didn't know him. All I knew was
there were over a dozen free library carrels—

I was the only one here on a Monday afternoon—
and he chose the carrel closest to me.

I had chosen the corner.
I like a pretense of quiet and space.

The man smiled at me but didn't hold my eyes,
then opened his Mac book two feet from mine.

I Googled "women's winter boots," wondering as it loaded
if perhaps I could move without appearing too rude,

and a small text appeared in a pale purple box
in the bottom right corner of my screen. An email:

This moment, LOVE comes to rest.
"This moment?" I thought.

Many beings in one being.
"Rumi?" I whispered, "Is that you?"

In one wheat-grain, a thousand sheaf stacks.
"It is you. But,"

Inside the needle's eye a turning night of stars.
And in between the carrel walls, between North Face

and Keen, between my annoyance and me
a thousand silences unfolded and for a few moments

I slid into the quiet that's been with me since before my birth.
Beyond mind. Beyond word. Beyond carols. Beyond hymn.

Rumi Enters the Sewing Room

Gr-RR-rrr-rrr-rrr, and it's tangled again,
the bobbin thread and the upper thread,
a mass of snarl beneath the felt mitten

and the needle won't budge one more stitch.
"Arhhh!" I shout to the midday air, and the room
answers back with its hush. "Why?" I say. "Why?"

And again I try the same thing: Rethread
the bobbin through the miniscule eye. Replace
the bobbin case in the shuttle hook, if that's

what it's called. I'm just reading the diagram,
after all. The parts may as well be called
Tuesday or toxic rain for how foreign they feel

in this moment when once again,
the eleventh time, I find myself threading
the bobbin and replacing the bobbin case

into the shuttle hook, if that's what it's called.
I press the pedal, and in four seconds flat
it's tangled again. And I slump. I hunch.

I mutter and blah. And Rumi tiptoes
up the carpeted stairs so I don't even know
that he's there behind me

till he breathes in my hair
and I jump. "Arhh!" It is hard
to let a mystic see me this way, with my

pulse elevated and my tongue full of curse
and he laughs. *Nibble,* he says. *Nibble
at me,* and I glare at him wishing

he'd just go away or say something practical,
like, "Dear Rosemerry, you just need
to slide the bobbin in clockwise."

But he doesn't. He says, *Don't gulp me down.*
What kind of advice is that? The mitten
is waiting. The boy who it's for has been

cutting lengthwise through all of my ribbons
while he waits for his mom to repair
the machine. *Nibble,* he says again to me.

And I force myself to breathe. It is only
because he is Rumi that I do not tell him
to leave. Instead, I think about taking

it slow and starting my process again.
"Nibble," I think. I breathe. "Not the bobbin
case. Think easier than that. Try again

the upper thread." For the first time
in half an hour, I try a new tack.
And I lace the thread through

the take up arm and the guide and the eye.
My foot finds the pedal. I try one more
time, "Hallelujah!" I cry as the stitches stitch on

and the mitten takes shape and Rumi,
jokingly sings, *How often is it*
you have a guest in your house

who can fix everything? I'm annoyed.
I'm elated. I turn to give him a kiss.
Rumi ducks and laughs and weaves

himself into the ribbon shreds,
the mitten thumb, the happy
mechanical humming.

Dark Night Still Life with Rumi

Silence.
Silence.
A howling hurt.
Silence. Silence.
Silence.

*

Outside, the crickets
continue to sing,
though they would
never think of it
as singing.

*

And Rumi says
to me,
How could we
know what an open
field of sunlight is?

*

Again I see
I do not know.
I don't know,
and the moon
hides.

*

But I want to know
where we are going.
Rumi says,
You are torturing
your soul.

*

Inside, still no moon.
But there is *a broken-*
open place.
I am learning
to sing from there.

Dear Rumi,

Sometimes I think if the night
were clear enough and the wind
were still, I could see
through all these walls I've built
to protect myself—from what?—
and know how to bring them down.
And then I could be open. But tonight
the sky could not be more clear
and there's no hint of wind
and I still feel in my heart
all the places still clenched and tight.

"Not open, dear, but opening,"
I imagine you might say, reminding me
that open is a verb, not some destination
where I might arrive—
some magical place with a beach and umbrella,
some anywhere I've dreamt up
that isn't wherever I am.

The prediction tomorrow
is snow, Rumi, and I will perhaps
be so enthralled or busy with it
that I will be drawn fully out of my thoughts
of open and opening and how.
But there I go again, planting myself
into the future as if it will be easier
to be present then than it is right now.

Right now, there's a knocking
in the kitchen. I don't know what it is.
A heater? The fridge?
And my own heart knocks
against my chest like a neighbor
who comes to borrow a cup of sugar
in the middle of the night.

I don't know, Rumi, why I am writing to you,
except that it feels as if something
has started in my soul, something
I don't understand. Something more
about forgetting than remembering.
And as you once said to your own teacher, Shams,
"You make my raggedness silky."

I turn to the yes I feel

when I read your words and know

that I know nothing. When I read you

it feels as if the angels that I don't quite believe in

have come, is that them doing all that knocking?

and those walls I mentioned, well,

I can almost laugh at them when the doors

I didn't even know were there

begin by themselves to open.

Gratitudes

One of the greatest pleasures of having a book of poems is the chance to say thank you to the many people who make life feel so rich, so full of potential and whose love, thoughts, words, support and presence find their way into these poems.

It was early summer when Markiah Friedman called to propose doing a book together. I was standing in the hot barn, painting a sign to put at our orchard entrance. Overwhelmed with thoughts of family and non-poetry work, putting together a collection of poems seemed so very unlikely. But his inspiration was contagious, and I thank him so much. What a beautiful, courageous idea to create a chapbook press dedicated to spiritually engaging poems. I honor his vision, appreciate his guidance, and I am so grateful to be included in Liquid Light's first year of publishing.

One of the biggest stumbling blocks was figuring out how to get permission to use the Rumi quotes that I was playing with in my poems. Um, ask? That's what my friend and favorite poetry editor, Kathryn T.S. Bass, helped me do. She emailed me a link to a Coleman Barks' website. How often do I not take step one because I am intimidated by what I think step three will look like? Thank you to Kathryn for this early encouragement, and also for her insightful editing skills.

My imagined "stumbling blocks" were exactly that. Imaginary. Big bouquets of gratitude to Coleman Barks and Daniel Ladinsky for their ecstatic renderings of Rumi's words into English—how they've changed my life! And thank you to them for their generous permission to reprint their translations in the context of these poems.

Part of what makes all of my writing possible is the graciousness of my husband, who supports me and helps me carve time for writing. Thank you, Eric.

And to Rumi, thank you for encouraging me to show up.

Notes and Permissions

For those who are not familiar with Jalal-ud-Din Rumi ...
here's a fine website full of information and resources for getting to
know him, *www.rumi.org.uk/life.html*

Rumi in the Garden
Rumi's quotes in this poem are adapted from "The Absolute Works
with Nothing," found in the HarperOne publication of *The Essential
Rumi.* Copyright © 2004 by Coleman Barks and used with his
permission.

Rumi Goes to the Beach
The quote in this poem comes from a dream.

Less
Rumi's quotes are excerpted from "Evening Sky Garnet Red," from
the HarperOne publication, *The Soul of Rumi.* Copyright © 2001 by
Coleman Barks and used with his permission.

Rumi Goes to Kindergarten
There is a poem circulating on the internet attributed to Rumi that
begins "Winter is a time for death. Do you think death is a bad
thing?" I have been unable to find a translator or title for this work.
The teacher in this poem, Rachel Lackey, was my son's kindergarten
teacher, who amazed me with her ability to mesmerize every child,
even the wildest, with her quiet, gentle demeanor.

Nine New Windows
The epigraph is from "The Guest House" found in the HarperOne
publication of *The Essential Rumi.* Copyright © 2004 by Coleman
Barks and used with his permission.

But Am I Ready?
The epigraph comes from "What Was Told, That" found in the
HarperOne publication, *The Soul of Rumi.* Copyright © 2001 by
Coleman Barks and used with his permission.

Rumi Appears at the Elementary Choir Concert
Rumi's quotes are from "With Passion," excerpted from the Penguin
publication, *Love Poems from God: Twelve Sacred Voices from the*

Life-lover, **Rosemerry Wahtola Trommer**, earned her master's degree in English Language and Linguistics. She served two terms as San Miguel County's first poet laureate and directs the Telluride Writers Guild. Her poems have been featured in *O Magazine* and on *A Prairie Home Companion,* and her books include *Holding Three Things at Once*, a finalist for the Colorado Book Award, *Intimate Landscape: The Four Corners in Poems & Photographs*, and *Charity: True Stories of Giving and Receiving*. Favorite four-word mantra: I am still learning. Favorite one-word mantra: Adjust.

CPSIA information can be obtained
at www.ICGtesting.com
Printed in the USA
BVHW081816080720
583188BV00003B/479